Potty Training In 3 Days

The Parent's Guide For Help Your Toddler to Leave the Diaper and Use the Potty. Includes Simple Tricks for Results in Very Few Days

Kate Cartes

© Copyright 2021 by Kate Cartes- All rights reserved.

The content contained within this book may not be reproduced, duplicated or transmitted without direct written permission from the author or the publisher.

Under no circumstances will any blame or legal responsibility be held against the publisher, or author, for any damages, reparation, or monetary loss due to the information contained within this book. Either directly or indirectly.

Legal Notice:

This book is copyright protected. This book is only for personal use. You cannot amend, distribute, sell, use, quote or paraphrase any part, or the content within this book, without the consent of the author or publisher.

Disclaimer Notice:

Please note the information contained within this document is for educational and entertainment purposes only. All effort has been executed to present accurate, up to date, and reliable, complete information. No warranties of any kind are declared or implied. Readers acknowledge that the author is not engaging in the rendering of legal, financial, medical or professional advice. The content within this book has been derived from various sources. Please consult a licensed professional before attempting any techniques outlined in this book.

By reading this document, the reader agrees that under no circumstances is the author responsible for any losses, direct or indirect, which are incurred as a result of the use of information contained within this document, including, but not limited to, errors, omissions, or inaccuracies.

Table of Contents

Introduction

Potty-training is one of those process parents employ in use with their kids to help them in managing their bowel movements for the benefit of both the parent and the child in the long run. In potty-training, parents try to teach the child to correctly recognize and communicate when he/she needs to use the bathroom, to resist the former urge of defecating where they are, and to use the potty or toilet properly.

In this book, we are going to take a look at some tips from those who have experienced it and can help you potty train your child quickly and efficiently. After all, they don't just learn it on their own. We have to be an inspiration and a model for them to follow!

Given the helpful tips that are provided in this guide, both you and your child will have the most positive experience with potty-training. Because all children are different in terms of their desire and ability to start using the toilet, you will need to make a plan that is flexible and nurturing.

With the use of positive reinforcement and creative techniques, your child will have the confidence that they need in order to learn all of the necessary steps. This success comes from your child's willingness to participate and your open-minded approach.

Getting rid of the pressure that surrounds the topic, you will learn if your child is ready by assessing their individual traits. It is important to remember that patience is the foundation of any milestone. The energy that you provide your child with is the energy that they are going to mirror. This is why staying calm and be patient is essential when you are potty-training. There are going to be some setbacks along the way, but if you are able to prepare yourself and your child adequately, you both will be able to overcome them with ease. Once you begin the process, you are already one step closer to achieving the potty-training goals.

Utilizing this guide, you are going to prepare a plan for your child to follow. As long as you are able to keep them on track and should start noticing the results right away. It is a milestone that every child is going to experience, and this book encourages the easiest method possible to ensure that potty-training will be accomplished without the stress of trying to get it done in a certain amount of time, you will both enjoy learning this next step together, and you will see that it can actually be fun!

Potty training your children isn't generally a pretty activity. Without a doubt, children virtually get bothered, so you should be cautious. Pretty things dependably get kids' attention. Consequently, you should make striking things that would get their attention. Presenting the training dynamically will surely shield your children from getting tired.

Is Your Child Ready to Roll?

This is, perhaps, the single most important question you need to ask before starting to focus your efforts on getting your child to use the potty!

Has your child demonstrated enough of the signs for you to try to start training? What are the signs of readiness? What's also important to note here is that readiness is needed on three different developmental levels in order to be successful quickly. Your child's physical, behavioral, and cognitive developments all play an important role in this adventure. If bladder control is an issue because the physical muscle development hasn't happened yet, then your child just isn't ready. However, if you notice that your child's diaper is dry at a time when you normally have to change it, you're probably looking at a child who is ready to train soon.

Your child needs the majority of these skills or milestones to be in place before you begin. Without these skills, your child really can't master all the steps in the potty training process.

This will leave you both tired and frustrated and can even lead to your child not wanting to potty train when they do have the ability.

CHAPTER 1:

Potty-Training in 3 Days

Potty-training your toddler can happen in three days but don't get frustrated if it doesn't work the first time. There are some rare toddlers who just aren't ready yet. However, if you believe your child is ready for potty-training, by all means, try this three-day method.

Some things to do with this training method are:

- Keep them naked from the waist down.

- Keep them in a restricted area close to the bathroom.

Day One: Learning What the Potty Is

On the first day, wake up your toddler, or wait until they decide to get up, then take them to the bathroom as soon as they get up. If you happen to catch them before they use their diaper, you can start off on the right foot and have them use the potty right away. However, don't be disappointed or upset if you don't get to them soon enough. You can move on to the following step.

The second step is to wait twenty minutes. You're going to take your toddler to the bathroom quite often throughout the day. It should be every twenty minutes, which is three times an hour. Take them to the bathroom, put them on their training potty, and tell them in a happy voice to go to the bathroom. Make sure you're positive! This shouldn't ever be a negative experience for your toddler.

They won't be able to pee every twenty minutes so, you're just teaching them to sit on the potty and try to go. They'll be able to go every couple of times, hopefully, or about every hour or two hours.

This might not occur on the first day. The idea is to get them to push and try every time they sit on the potty. They should have gone once or twice by the end of your first day. Even a little bit of pee when they sit down is amazing progress! You're helping them avoid an accident by giving them many chances to use the bathroom.

You don't have to praise them insanely every time they sit on the potty. If they try but don't happen to produce anything, tell them, "Good try." Every time they sit down is helpful in terms of teaching them how to use the bathroom. Save your excited praise for the actual event. You want them to be excited when you're excited because this gives them the motivation to keep trying to use the bathroom.

When they begin peeing on the floor (and they will), run over to them as soon as you see it happen. Pick them up and take them to the potty to use it. When you see them beginning to pee on the floor, tell them, "Pee-pee doesn't go on the floor, it goes in the potty!" Do this every time. This is the reason you should restrict their space and keep them naked.

Being on the other side of the house, away from the potty, when this happens it will be difficult to handle. On the other hand, being only a few steps away from the bathroom will make this process a lot easier, as they'll still be peeing when you get them to the potty. Praise them if they end up getting a few dribbles in the potty. This will reinforce the idea of peeing in the potty.

For example, if you catch your toddler beginning to pee on the floor, pick them up quickly and tell them that pee goes in the potty. Take them a few steps to the potty and sit them down so they can finish in the training potty. When they finish, that's a success! Cheer and smile; show your toddler the pee in the training potty. Then have them help you carry that to the potty and flush it. Showing them the flushing of their urine reinforces the idea that this is normal.

It's important to have your toddler wash their hands with you and to tell them you're proud of them for going to the bathroom on the potty. Then go back to the designated area and show them where they went on the floor. Tell them that they don't pee on the floor, it's gross, and that pee goes in the potty. Point to the potty, then clean up the mess. Repeat this for three days. If they don't go again within twenty minutes, take them to the potty and have them try to go and repeat this every twenty minutes.

Now that you have demonstrated to them what will happen, you must keep it up! That means every twenty minutes for the entire day for three days. They should be naked all throughout the day, except for naptime and bedtime. Nighttime potty-training is different from daytime potty-training.

Consider it a success if your toddler attempts to go to the potty, pees on the potty or acknowledges that he has had an accident when he pees running down their legs. This is going to be the case for most kids, starting around the middle of the first day. Every child will be different; their personalities are different, so the rate at which they learn to go on the potty will be different. Some will be trained within a day or two, while others will need a few more days to practice.

Day Two: Accident-Free Time

On the first day, your toddler doesn't really get the idea, but they'll learn that they need to go to the bathroom on the potty and not on the floor. On the second day, you'll be expanding on that idea, helping them grasp it. By the second day, most kids will almost completely stop having accidents and will use the potty about seventy percent of the time.

If your toddler is using the potty more than half the time, it's safe to take them from going to the potty every twenty minutes to going to the potty every half an hour to forty minutes. If you feel that they'd benefit from a second day of every-twenty-minutes, by all means, go for it. It'll only help your toddler, not hinder them. Two days of every-twenty-minutes should be enough to get the idea to sink into your child's mind; however, if they aren't making it after two days, you might want to think about holding off for a few more weeks and trying again in the future.

If you really feel up to it, you can try the every-twenty-minutes method for a third day. You're using the same idea as on day one, but increasing the amount of time between trips. You still need to stay in the potty-training area, especially if they're having a lot of accidents. If they're using the potty on-demand or not experiencing accidents, this might work. They'll still have some accidents, so keep that in mind when you decide to expand their area.

Remember, keep your toddler in a diaper at night and during naptime. Sleep potty-training will take some time, and while it can be done, you're already going to be exhausted from trying to complete daytime potty-training in three days. Don't overwhelm yourself or your toddler. If you're feeling up to it, you can try it now, but never get upset or angry if your child continues to have nighttime accidents. Some toddlers aren't nighttime trained until they're well above the age of two.

Day Three: Increase the Time

On the third day, you can try to have your toddler go every hour rather than every half an hour. They should still be naked in the morning. You'll still want to keep them in their confined area, such as on a single floor of your home if there are two stories, or close to some bedroom doors if you're in a single-story home or apartment. Keep them close, but you don't have to stay in the close quarters as you were in before. Keep taking your toddler to the potty every hour, or more often if you have to. Your toddler should be using the potty and not having many accidents now if you're able to catch them on time.

You're going to miss a few accidents, but that's all right. Halfway through this day, when you feel pretty confident that your toddler is getting the idea, you can move them into underwear. This is going to be difficult for them to understand and it's when you're going to want to give up because it feels like a diaper for them.

It's a little confusing for them, so you need to stay on top of them to look for signs that they need to go. Pee running down their legs or pee in their underwear are both signs that you should get them to the potty quickly. Also, do this if they start to take off their underwear. Your toddler is going to have a few accidents on this day. They'll begin peeing in their underwear. They might look sad about this or they might not care at all, but you should stick with it. Don't give up!

Some toddlers really struggle with the concept of underwear. When you put the underwear on them, they immediately begin peeing in it. Your toddler might feel like the underwear is a diaper. Sometimes, you might have to leave them in their clean underwear and take them to the potty every twenty minutes to help them get used to the feel. Do this for the entire third day.

You can extend the potty-training another day or two. When the third day comes to a close, remember that you'll be in the training stage for about a month. However, your toddler should understand the basic concept of going potty on the toilet and not in their underwear or diaper. They probably won't have an accident if you're on top of it, such as by taking them to the potty every hour or so. You'll know how often your toddler has to go, so be sure to take them during those times.

For the first few weeks, you'll want to keep your toddler naked from the waist down as much as possible until you feel confident that they won't be having any additional accidents. If you're home, keep them naked or in their underwear at all times, for around a month. It's still going to be weeks or months before your toddler lets you know they have to go without being reminded. They may not have accidents during this time, but they could hold their pee until you take them to go.

Take them every hour or so for a few hours, regardless of whether they show signs of needing to go, this way you will eliminate accidents. If you need to go out, remember that your child should go to the bathroom before you leave, and then again when you arrive wherever you're going. You might want to take them a little more often to avoid accidents outside the home during those first few months.

Don't leave home without your travel potty. If you don't want to take your toddler to the potty where you're going, have them go with the travel potty before you get out of the car.

Here's a huge reminder for all parents who are potty-training their toddler in three days – it's difficult for your toddler to tell you when they have to go because they don't recognize the sensation yet, so you need to watch for signs from them that they need to use the potty. These signs could be holding themselves, trying to hide, or dancing around. Remember, they'll most likely learn when they need to pee by having a few accidents on the floor or in their underwear, and then they'll realize that urine is coming out.

CHAPTER 2:

Getting Rid of Diapers During Sleeping Hours

Babies and toddlers who receive good toilet training will eventually internalize the new skill properly and stop experiencing misses altogether during waking – as well as – sleeping hours. From that point on they simply cease to eliminate their bodily secretions in their clothing, day and night. Gladly and luckily, we can say that this type of internalization occurs in the large majority of children. Over 75% quit bedwetting by the time they are four years old. This type of spontaneous weaning relieves many parents of the long and weary burden of dealing with night-time toilet training. If your child belongs to this majority you will see that soon after your child has grasped the idea, diapers will be dry in the morning. At that point, you could safely remove the diaper and put your child to sleep in regular cloth underwear.

The remaining minority of children continue to wet their bed in their sleep: about 15% of all six-year-old, 8% of all ten years old, and 5% of all twelve years old have trouble with night-time urine control. For general information, night-time wetting is considered a problem when it lasts after the age of five, and by then it is recommended to seek therapy.

Night-Time Weaning – From Dream to Reality

Every educational or disciplinary process, toilet-training included, should be initiated, managed, run and guided by the parents who accept full and sole responsibility for its execution including timing, stages, strategies, implementation, and results. Parents (and not children.) set the goals, take the measures needed for these goals to be achieved, and guide their children, hand in hand, while providing leadership and support, all the way to the process's successful conclusion.

True, we expect that at the end of this educational process, the child, who has already learned to control bodily needs during waking hours, will learn to stretch the new skill to night time as well. However, as an initial goal, for many parents, it will suffice to find a happy child in a dry bed every morning, not really caring whether the credit for this achievement belongs to them or to their child.

In other words, if you wake up your child at night, once or twice, in order to go to the toilet, it is all right and a good thing, especially at the beginning of the 'dry-night' training process. As long as your child does not wet the bed and manages to wake up dry in the morning, let me assure you that you have achieved your goal, at least for now. In addition, your child may actually benefit from your help, emotionally. Let me remind you again, that the process stays under your sole responsibility, as parents, until your child has internalized the desired behavior. Only then you could gradually pass on the responsibility, decreasing the scope of your help one inch at a time.

Some people may claim that if you help your child to go to the toilet at night then your child is not really weaned from the diaper. I, on the other hand, claim that it does not matter at all. As long as your child wakes up dry, a fact which is welcomed by all parties involved no matter their age, we have certainly got us an achievement and quite a significant one too. The child's self-pride, and its contribution to his or her self-esteem, absolutely justify your efforts as parents. Moreover, I believe that the mere fact that we find a way to avoid bed-wetting, and manage to maintain it for a long period of time, serves to separate the child from the undesired behavior. What I mean to say is that the child does not realize that the possibility of releasing bodily needs in the bed even exists.

These are the following steps you need to take in order to wean your child from diapers at night:

- Preferably end all eating and drinking sessions an hour before sleeping time

- Make it a habit to go to the toilet as the last thing you do before going to bed, after storytime, cuddle time, and all other going to sleep rituals.

- Remind your child, every night, to be bladder-conscious; meaning that you make sure that your child knows to associate internal pressure on the bladder, even during sleep, with going to the toilet. If your child is not independent yet and cannot go alone, make sure that it is known that you are available to offer help no matter the hour. You can tell your child something like: when you sleep, and you feel like you need to pee, don't pee in bed. Wake yourself up, call me, and I will take you to the bathroom.

- Wake up your child by your own initiative: If your child does not wake up at night to go to the bathroom, and is not able to hold the urine until morning, then explain that in order to help him or her keep dry at night you will take him or her to the toilet to pee. When you wake up your child, do whatever you can to maintain the night time atmosphere.

Don't raise your voice, it is OK to whisper. You can whisper to your child something like: "Honey, wake up, it's time to go to the bathroom and pee". Help your child get up and walk but make sure your child is aware of what is happening. After peeing in the bathroom whisper something like: "Well done, you just peed in the bathroom. Now we can go back to sleep".

Accumulated parental experience will teach you, the parents, when would be the best time to wake up your child to go to the toilet at night. It is, again, a process of trial and error. You will eventually learn which hours are best to take your child to the bathroom at night. Some parents wake up their children for this purpose right before they go to sleep. Others may learn that an additional toilet-session is needed sometime around the early morning hours. Make sure that your child wakes up and walks to the toilet independently and is not taken by you in deep sleep. Your child should be awake and aware, at least partially, when this happens. Of course, the whole thing should last no more than several minutes; no extra lights, no talking, no partying, and as calmly as possible. It is certainly OK to say a good word of encouragement or praise when all is done and then go right back to bed.

Often, this kind of parental intervention helps children go through the transitional phase from dependency on the diaper to control and independence during night time. This transitional phase may last several months too, and sometimes even years. This does not mean that it is not working; only that in some educational processes, for some children, time is essential in order to provide a positive and effective learning experience.

Appreciation must be expressed to the many parents who are willing to sacrifice the quality of their sleep in order to help their children overcome night-time bedwetting. I must say, though, that occasionally I run into parents who admit that they prefer to diaper their children during the night because it is too hard for them to wake up. Sometimes, once a night is not enough and accidents occur despite the parents' efforts. Those parents not only sacrifice their good night's sleep but also find themselves struggling with huge amounts of laundry, and with a sleeping child in a wet bed, who needs changing every night. I appreciate their honesty, I can surely sympathize with their discouragement, but seeing the big picture and the long-term goal, I cannot say that I can second their decision.

If Nothing Works

Sometimes there can be medical explanations that should be ruled out, but as far as we know, these cases do not exceed two percent of all cases of children with this problem.

The common professional approach today categorizes the difficulties in night time weaning as caused by a natural delay in the child's physiological-neurological development, which is the reason for the dysfunction of the reflex system which controls the bladder. In simple words: the pressure on the bladder fails to wake the child before the urine is released; thereby the urine is released while the child is still asleep. Some children do not even wake up despite the wetness which spreads around them.

In most cases (75-80%), the problem is attributed to the lack of maturity of the nervous system and the wetting is described and defined as a disability to learn how to hold.

This is all good and well, but before you become alarmed and freaked out with these long-worded medical explanations I want you to know that sometimes very simple changes on your part can make a huge and unexpected difference in progress. If nothing else, it is worth your try.

When we are dealing with an older child, around the ages of four and five and even older, who continues – whether on a regular basis or even occasionally – to wake up in a wet bed, despite sleep-time toilet trips, then I believe that it is time to take your disciplinary seriousness one notch up. Under these circumstances it is OK to expect your child to take responsibility for the outcome; and by that I do not mean that you should punish or embarrass your child in any way but rather that you can and should demand his or her help taking care of the results – meaning, changing sheets, cleaning up and changing clothes, and even doing the laundry, as long as it is done in a way that matches their age and ability.

Children are able to understand that their action or lack of it has consequences that affect them. I believe that letting your child experience the consequences first-hand is educationally justified. Of course, you should help, but it will do no harm if your child understands that changing bed sheets and clothing is his or her responsibility too and that they are not exempt from dealing with the mess they created.

Experience has proved that many children who used to wet their bed regularly stopped once they experienced the hassle and discomfort of cleaning up in the morning. So long as they did not have to deal with the consequences of their doing, they continued to wet their bed. Let us be honest: why should they invest any efforts if Mommy alone cleans up after them? The minute parents become less lenient and demand that their children take an active part in the cleaning many children prefer to align themselves with the new standards.

CHAPTER 3:

Naptime Training and Nighttime Training

Nighttime potty training is the second half of potty training and most often does not happen directly after successful daytime toilet training. It is normal for children to be fully potty trained in the daytime, but not yet be able to control things during the night. The most important thing is to not force nighttime toilet training on your child. Let their bodies develop enough, and look for the readiness signs before you start nighttime training.

Day vs. Night Potty Training

Parents should understand that nighttime training is not simply a continuation of daytime potty training. Look at it as a completely different step. When potty training for daytime, your child is fully awake and alert and can communicate with you. You are also able to read their body language during the day and see the signs that alert you to the fact that they need the potty or the toilet.

Nighttime potty training is complicated because your child must develop bladder control strong enough to be able to hold it in during their sleep. They must also be able to wake up from a deep sleep, meaning their bodies must signal them strong enough that they need the toilet to actually wake them up. They must then be awake enough to walk to the bathroom and afterward return to their beds. This is a lot of things to learn to do successfully during times when their minds are not fully awake.

When to Start

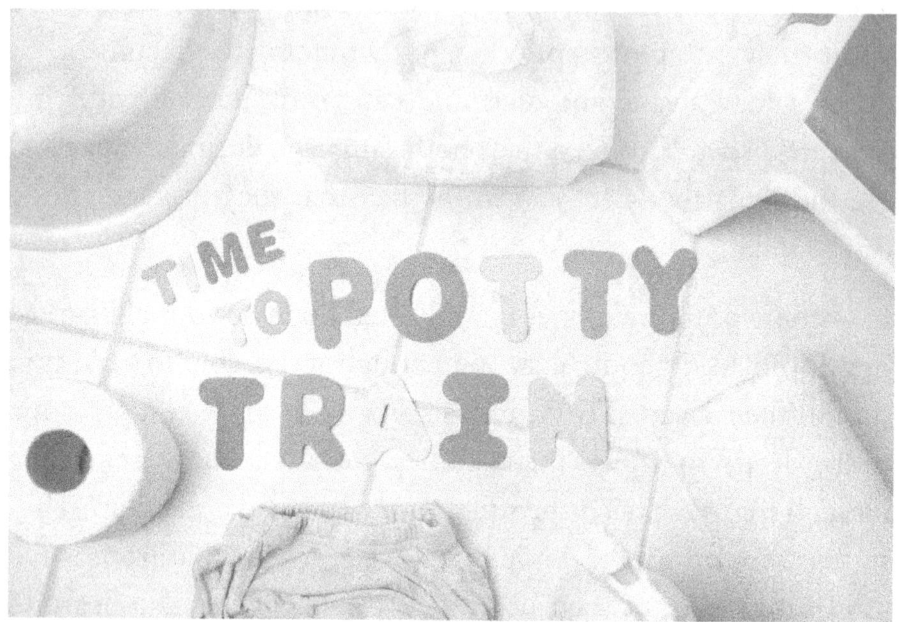

When you think it is time to start and you and your child are ready, the first thing to look at is what is happening at home at that moment. Has there been any recent changes that caused upheaval? Are there any travel plans coming up? Or, have you recently or are about to move home? These are very important things as changes affect young children very much, even if they don't have the vocabulary to express it properly.

Make sure that when you want to start, everything is normal at home and that your child has an established nighttime routine. This stability is needed so that nighttime potty training slips into their routine without causing any disruption.

Sometimes parents get lucky and their toddler will tell them that he or she thinks they want to wear big kid pants to bed and not nappies. This is a golden opportunity parents should grab with both hands. You need your child's cooperation and when they prompt this move to nighttime potty training, be sure that you are ready and prepared for it. Have everything needed in place and start immediately.

The norm, however, is that parents have to watch for the signs that their child is ready. For nighttime training, this means your child must already be fully daytime potty trained, and they are at the stage where you find that their nighttime nappies are often dry in the morning. You may also find that they have gone several nights in a row without having a wet nappy in the morning.

Parents should be aware that children often use their nighttime nappy for that first pee in the morning when they wake up, and this is a natural thing to do. So, add that into the equation when considering whether your child is ready or not.

If you think the time is right and if your child is about 3 ½ years old you can have a subtle conversation with them about no longer using diapers or pull-ups at night. Explain that you think that they are ready to start going to the toilet, or use their potty at night. Keep it low-key without any pressure on the child and see if this starts the process. If not, give it a rest for a few weeks and then try again.

How Long Does This Phase Last?

There is no time limit, age limit, duration limit for nighttime potty training. Each child will nighttime train according to his or her physical readiness. One thing many pediatricians agree on is that there should be a definite gap between daytime and nighttime training. Some children will go through the nighttime training in a matter of a few weeks, while others literally take a few years.

It is not possible to give an average time that nighttime toilet training takes because of the numerous factors that have to be taken into consideration. Even with twins, you will find that they will take a different amount of time and most likely will not start nighttime training at the same time either.

A very broad guideline, without factoring in all the personal aspects, is that children are typically daytime potty trained between the ages of 2 and 4. By the ages of 5 or 6, the majority of them are nighttime toilet trained with the nighttime training phase lasting from a few months to a few years.

Be Prepared

Most parents are fully prepared long before they start potty training their child and have thought of all the different supplies and equipment they will need. With nighttime potty training, there are a few very specific supplies that parents should get before they start training. Some of these are not absolute essentials, but worth investigating as options that can make everything just that much easier.

Bedwetting Alarm

This is not an essential item but can be a help when you are nighttime potty training an older toddler, or if nighttime training does take place over a long period of time. These alarms work best for children who are able to go to the toilet on their own as extra help as these alarms help them to wake up when they start urinating.

These alarms are designed to assist when children experience bedwetting problems but are great to have for nighttime training. If your child does not wake up from the alarm easily, it will alert a parent who then can easily take the child to the toilet.

Disposable Diapers

It is always good to have a stack of disposable nappies at hand for nighttime training for those extra accidents that crop up and easy changing of a very sleepy child.

Extra Blankets/Duvets

Make sure that you have at least one extra duvet and a few blankets available to do bed changes in the shortest possible time and the minimum of fuss. The sooner the bed is changed, the sooner tired parents can get back to bed as well.

Extra Sheets

Extra sheets are an absolute must for nighttime potty training. You simply never have too many sheets, and it is a good idea to opt for fitted sheets if possible. (See tips and tricks for using sheets).

Light Switch Extender

Little people most often cannot reach light switches easily. The adult world simply does not cater to those short legs and small hands. See what types of light switch extenders are available in your local area to check them out and the various different functions they may have. The first place you place a light switch extender is the bathroom, to give your little one that extra bit of independence when they want to go use the potty or toilet on their own at night.

Pull up training pants are the way many parents go for nighttime toilet training. You can bring an element of fun into this by letting your little one choose to pull up pants with designs of their favorite characters on them. Having their favorite characters on the training pans could be a motivation for them to not pee or poop in the pants.

Waterproof Mattress Protectors

Mattress protectors and mattress pads come in a huge variety of styles and prices to suit everyone. Look for a protector that is hypoallergenic and machine washable. Read the specs of the different mattress protectors that you are interested in, as some are guaranteed to block dust mites, mildew, and mold as well. Another spec to look for is whether it is designed to regulate sleep temperature and airflow. If you can, get two so you are always ready, even if one protector is in the wash.

Disposable Sheet Liners

These are handy to have and help with many bedwetting accidents. Some may say that having mattress protectors and disposable sheet liners is overkill, but that is for each parent to decide to what extent they want to protect their little one's bed and bedding.

Tips and Tricks

Liquids

You need to put some rules in place regarding liquids otherwise nighttime potty training will not work. You have to limit water and juice intake late in the day and during the evening.

Make it a rule that they have the last liquid at suppertime and after that only small sips of water, milk, or juice. Instead, concentrate on hydrating them as much as possible during the day. Let the child have as much liquid as they want, and do many potty or toilet sessions as needed during the day.

What often helps to lessen late liquid intake is to get them a very small cup. Look for a cute cup that they will like that holds only a little liquid and explain that this is their special evening cup, only for them.

Lights

Lights are important for nighttime potty training. No toddler will go to the toilet in darkness. The solution is to install a nightlight in your child's bedroom. There are so many different types to choose from that you might find it difficult to choose. Many parents pick a night light that will be soothing for their child and help them drift off to sleep.

Another option is to leave the bathroom light on so that your child can easily find their way there and back to bed. A night light also benefits the parent who checks on the little one during the night as switching on overhead light is not a great idea as it could wake up your sleeping child.

Bedtime Routine

Routines are part of everyone's life and getting that last potty session done before your child gets into bed can be easily incorporated into his or her bedtime routine. Make it part of the routine of brushing teeth and whatever else you already have for the bedtime routine. You can also have a double potty session before bedtime, for instance, by having a potty time about 30 minutes before bedtime and then the last one just before getting into bed.

Last Bathroom Stop

Many parents find it very helpful in their nighttime potty training efforts to get their little one to go to the toilet just before they themselves get into bed. Usually, parents are awake for at least 3 hours after the child goes to bed, so it is a good time to take your sleepy little one to the toilet and help to hold your child propped up on the potty or toilet for that extra pee if possible.

Bed Protection

Mattress protectors and disposable sheet liners have been discussed in the section of getting prepared for nighttime potty training. A good tip for parents that experience many accidents during the night is to make up their child's bed by layering sheets and waterproof pads. If parents have several sheets and waterproof pads or disposable sheet liners over one another it makes stripping the bed in the middle of the night very easy. Just remove the solid sheet and liner, and it can be put a little one straight back into bed.

CHAPTER 4:

Behavior vs Potty Training

Firstly, I have to cover some ground on the subject of boundaries and limits; after that, I'll hit particular behaviors I've seen in potty schooling. Boundaries and limitations have a poor rep in parenting lately. They can appear mean or draconian or too authoritarian. Many parents don't have confidence in any consequence or discipline. I want to state outright: I do not advocate, nor do I believe in hitting or beating a kid ever.

Certainly, the first couple of days, and maybe actually the first couple of weeks, are filled with learning. Learning, naturally, requires making some errors and/or having some incidents. However, there exists a difference between learning and behavior or habit. When your kid is showing behavior, and after all of the poor variety, the behavior must be addressed.

You are potty training around the two-year age range, and around the same time, you might see various other two-year-old behavior. This might well be the first time you are seeing your child act, but it's normal. The awful twos aren't only a cliché; they are real. Throughout normal development, your son or daughter must test limitations. It's his work. He needs to find out where the fence is, as they say. The reason your wall in your backyard is there is indeed not to make your child wander and get misplaced. Limits and boundaries will be the fence in your child's psyche. With them intact, just while in your backyard, your child feels safe and sound, knowing where he may go and may not go.

A trend in contemporary parenting is to assume that the kid is with the capacity of deciding good stuff for himself without having to be provided any boundaries or limits. That is not the case. I frequently look to the Montessori system for how exactly to allow children to make some decisions while also providing boundaries. Within a framework, the kids are absolved from making choices; however, they are not free to carry out whatever it is they need.

The children all consume lunch collectively. You can't make a couple of kids get a snack in the fridge and leave this up to them to choose if they are hungry, it could lead to mayhem. The kids all go outside jointly, whether one is tired or not really. Our children need some boundaries. Within those boundaries, we can enable tremendous freedom.

What I see, both from my experience and in my work is that most of us parents have a problem with providing freedom within boundaries? In our quest to improve free-thinking, kids are not offered enough framework to allow them to feel safe.

Imagine the stress your child would feel if you were driving, been at the backseat, and he or she has no idea of where you were heading. I've extrapolated that idea even more. Imagine if your son or daughter were responsible for providing you the directions, and which you followed their instructions. Proceed left. Go right. No. Stop. Wow. You'd quickly be lost, yes? That's where points will get mucky with the oft-touted child-led style of parenting. You could be child-led for the reason that you pay attention to and validate your son or daughter's opinion, but you just can't follow your child's lead through life.

All this is especially true in case you have a spirited or strong-willed child. I frequently work with parents who have a kid fitting this explanation. This child is generally demanding and will be challenging with regard to potty training as well. Still, this child requires boundaries and limits just as much as, or even more than, your garden-variety child.

All well and great, but what does this need to do with potty training?

Well, occasionally behavior kicks up during potty teaching. And because potty schooling is so wrought with emotion, it becomes hard to draw it aside from behavior. I also discover that parents will endure all types of behavior during potty schooling that they wouldn't work in other circumstances.

For example, one of the primary challenges parents today encounter during potty training gets their child to take a seat on the potty. Yes, you can go through to them or sing to them. I state it's all right to play with a mobile device seeing that as a distraction in the beginning. But, when you inquire your son or daughter to sit to go potty, your son or daughter should sit. Today, to a lot of individuals that sounds severe.

You show your son or daughter to sit and they don't. How can you handle that?

I'm requesting because-whatever your response is, that's how you're likely to handle it during potty training. When it's supper, it's time to sit and consume. When it's potty period, it's time to take a seat on the potty.

Once you encounter behavior during potty training, do your very best to put it right into a different context. That will assist you to figure out how better to deal with it in the context of potty schooling. It's your parenting duty. I do not really nor have I ever comfy telling people the way to handle behavior generally. That's why I'm providing you a framework to work with, and you may make your own parenting decisions.

Many parents say, "We don't feel safe making him sit." I agree. I don't believe you should force your son or daughter to sit. Nevertheless, it's worth pondering precisely how fearful we are because of the potty. Many parents dread doing anything unfavorable around potty training. Utilizing a firm or stern voice seems contrary to these parents, and they're worried about traumatizing the kid. This is where another scenario will come in handy. Everyone has held their kid down and strapped them in the car seat. Even though they are kicking, screaming, and hitting. We perform it because we should go somewhere, and we need them to be safe. Has your son or daughter ever been traumatized by that rather than wished to sit in the automobile front seat someday? I'm guessing no. Again, I'm not saying you should exert pressure on your child onto the potty or strap him down, or anything remotely like this. I'm simply pointing out that fear of traumatizing a kid by conveying the message that you mean the business has gotten a bit out of control.

If your son or daughter shows a particular "problem"- say he's whiny, or she's resistant or susceptible to histrionics and tantrums, you will have this same kid if you are potty teaching. No judgment; there is absolutely no behavior I've not really seen. Still, I discover parents who in some way think potty training will happen in a bubble in which the rest of the behavior the kid exhibits is somehow not likely to appear even though it's potty training. That is a big transition, so these behaviors can not only be right there, but they may get magnified for a brief period. Again, it's all great. Just keep your anticipations level as well as your love big.

Whatever your child's personality is, I can't change that or correct it; that's built-in the child's physiology. If your son or daughter is exhibiting the behavior you do not like, or you are feeling is usually disrespectful, you will likely see that same behavior during potty schooling. What I could tell you is how exactly to deal with a few of the behaviors you find in potty training.

Here's a clear exemplary case of behavior. Say your son or daughter did ideal for a couple of days. Suddenly, they don't want to utilize the potty anymore. This may appear to be a defiant "NO." or it could seem they just can't be bothered with this. If he or she sat and peed/pooped on the potty several times, then we realize that they can perform it, it's that easy. If they subsequently choose never to, it's behavior.

In case you are feeling unfortunate or just a little heartbroken that it isn't heading as you intended, it's likely that your son or daughter needs more learning. If you feel as if you are being pranked, if you feel anger, or if you feel like strangling your kid, I'll wager its behavior. Usually, parents have a pervasive sense when they are coping with behavior but don't carry out anything because they're terrified of "traumatizing" the kid.

Having boundaries and pursuing through won't traumatize your kid in any sense. When you have a youngster whom you understand is taking part in you, the very best move to make is to provide a small, instant, appropriate consequence. For example, take away the play toy he was using when he wet his slacks, or consider restraining him from the activity where he was involved.

The small, immediate consequence can be helpful when you aren't sure whether he needs more learning or is exhibiting the behavior. I believe I've managed to get clear that satisfaction and self-mastery ought to be the motivation behind potty training a child effectively. However, for a few children that by no means clicks in, plus they need some exterior motivation to nudge things along. Some parents react such as, "But I'll feel terrible if I provide him a consequence, and he needs even more learning." Removing a little toy consequently won't scar your child forever. And it's the quickest way to get a remedy. If your child can't utilize the potty realizing that his toy is sure to get placed on the fridge for one hour if he doesn't, you can wager that so far, he needs more to learn, and he won't be scared. If your child can do it all, you then know the incidents are because of behavior. I'm talking about real-world potty training, not theory. Effects are sure to get you your solution the fastest.

Some parents say, "Isn't a consequence only the opposite of an incentive? I'd rather give incentive for the behavior I want rather than provide a consequence for what we don't want." I am aware of the idea behind this and, yes, generally, positive reinforcement is most effective with children. Nevertheless, we get back to that notion of expected behavior. The problem with benefits and potty schooling is that they get sticky. The stakes must be continuously raised to ensure they work. If you are likely to reward for peeing, where else can that lead? I'd rather curb undesired behavior than prize the hell out of excellent behavior. Else, you finish up with a youngster who expects to end up being rewarded for everything.

I fully have confidence in the benefits of exemplary behavior, and I also think that bad behavior gets a consequence.

CHAPTER 5:

Bedwetting, a Potty-Training Challenge

A most likely reason is a developmental delay, biology (even here), sleep disturbance (like sleeping too deep), mental disorders, and psychological, anti-diuretic hormone levels.

Causes of Bedwetting

The most often recognized cause of primary nocturnal enuresis, but also the most difficult to prove is the maturation lag of the central nervous system. Mainly, the infant's nervous system does not believe that the bladder has to be held, and the urine discharges during sleep.

Sleeping conditions affect substantial percentages of children who suffer from bedwetting, and extensive research has been carried out on the matter. Still, the findings have been so varied that it is difficult for researchers to identify a primary sleep disorder that can be defined as the leading cause of litter.

Some people think that bedwetting is primarily behavioral, contributing to the question of emotional concern. Some studies have shown that emotionally, children suffering from nighttime enthusiasts have precisely the same conduct as children who don't. In these studies, that demonstrate psychological distinctions between the two groups, the main differences were that a child with a bedwetting problem was socially less and had more self-esteem problems than the other group. It raises the question: do low self-esteem and social issues go hand in hand with nursing babies or do nursing contribute to these kinds of mental situations?

Family history is essential, and several studies have shown results that it seems almost conclusive that when a parent has had a child's bed weather, their child is likely to have very high chances. One study showed a 77 percent chance in a family in which both parents had the same disease. It helps to dissipate the theory that enuresis is a behavioral problem. It, in effect, makes it more appropriate and induces somewhat less stress and shame, leading to better outcomes following treatment.

Treatment of Bedwetting

You can try different ways to deal with a bedwetting condition without the intervention of a doctor or medical attention. Whether or not a medical procedure is mainly required depends on many factors: such as the age of a child, how often they wet the bed, and the seriousness perceived by the family of the child. Most children do outgrow bedwetting and need no physician treatment at all for it.

Many parents utilize bedwetting wall pads at night, and although they do a great job in preventing the bed from moisture due to the accident, they do very little to resolve the problem. While concentrating on its aspect of bedwetting is very important; trying to prevent future events is also extremely important. It is why it is good to use many essential methods of prevention as early as possible. So, you may decide to take your child to your doctor if they don't function. However, you should know that children under the age of six are generally not treated by doctors if the only problem is bed weeping.

Once you have chosen to bring your child to a doctor about bedwetting, it is essential to know that the ultimate goal of entirely accident-free nights can take a long time to reach. The parent and the child must remain committed to this long process. There are two techniques that doctors use to address bedwetting problems: medicine and behavioral therapy. Parents and children must be as cooperative as possible to try their doctor's advice. If anyone has a bad attitude, solving the problem can be much more difficult, if not impossible.

The doctor likely wants to remove all medical conditions at the very start. Although most kids seen by doctors are perfectly healthy in bedwetting, some have a medical condition. So, before a doctor approaches it as if they don't, they want to make sure it is true. The doctor's evaluation of your child should be targeted to exclude anatomical abnormalities of the urinary bladder or tract. These may involve conditions like postural urethral valves, an ectopic ureter, or an episodic urethra that is an opening of the urethra of the penis' dorsum.

When the doctor undertakes a thorough examination, which involves a family medical history, physical examination, and urine analysis, he or she can usually determine whether there is a medical condition and, if so, what the disorder could be. If your child is treated for enuresis and even before, it is an excellent idea to keep a record of incidents of bedwetting. In addition to its dairy, it is great to write down anything that could have occurred that day to disturb the child's natural emotional equilibrium if the bedwetting of the baby does not happen repetitively at night.

When you determine whether or not there is a medical condition that contributes to your child's bedwetting situation, you can see which methods of treatment help you best. It is worth noting that coherent take-up could be a key to improving bed weathering (it is also worth knowing that most doctors usually describe improvements as a decline in bedwetting regularity of 50%).

Your physician may choose to use only one or both methods of treatment together. The therapeutic strategies may and typically include an alarm system, a recompense system, demanding your child to switch sheets, and bladder training.

Bedwetting alarms can be a useful tool to help your baby retrain the sleep patterns so that he or she sleep better and wake up a little more often during the night. You can schedule them for some time to get your child up and try to use them anytime the alarm goes off.

A reward system can also be a useful behavioral therapy tool, particularly when the child has developed new patterns of sleep and has less frequent injuries. Giving a small bonus each day after a dry night or a large prize at the end of a particular duration, including a whole week of dry nights, can give your child even more incentive to wake up at night.

Changing the bedding for your baby is also a great way to prevent them from getting as many bedding nights. Although it's not fair to punish a child for anything they can't control, it is not punishment, and it's a way for them to understand that, even when they are asleep, they have to take responsibility for their actions. It also works well because they have to get out of bed and sleep more often, which can, in effect, make them sleep better regularly.

One type of behavioral therapy is bladder training, which can help reduce bed weeping nights. That is because your child holds its bladder for longer and longer periods during the day. You may always go to the toilet when you feel the urge to go, and so when you fall into a deep sleep, your body reacts when it reaches you. When you teach your child to keep it for as long as they can when the urge arrives while awake, they are more likely to be able to resist it subconsciously while asleep.

If behavioral therapy does not work and medicines can only be prescribed if the child is seven years old. Medications work best in behavioral treatment, as it is not a bedwetting solution. They can also have side effects. If you decide to use drugs to treat your child, use one prescribed by your doctor. It helps the bladder to maintain more urine and reduces the urine in the kidneys. These are not the kinds of medication you want your child to use regularly throughout their lives.

It's not only you'll try to help your child overcome their bedwetting dilemma, but you should also focus on assisting them in understanding it and, if possible, don't feel so bad about it. Your child probably feels very ashamed of being in bed. You may also feel guilty that you can't control your body in the way you think you can. For older children, it is very likely. It's a problem; you should never punish your child. It is essential to remember that your baby can not prevent it. The older the child is, the more so, and your child is probably more irritated than you are. You try not to make your child feel guiltier about it than they do.

It can also help your child know that nobody knows the cause of bedwetting exactly because each case has too many factors to consider. Tell them about the many various objects that could impact their condition and the fact that they are not responsible for these reasons, and that you help them overcome it. Tell them all the knowledge they need to help them do so without thinking less of themselves. For example, when you wet the bed as a baby, be sure to explain and remind them that it could run in families. It could help to relieve some of the pressure and some of your remorse.

Remember, it's hard for you and your child to use any means necessary to clean up your bedwetting problems. The correct no-fault attitude can help and open your mind to treatment suggestions and be committed to any way you decide to treat sleeping weathering and potty training.

CHAPTER 6:

Potty Training Away From Home

I need you to understand that when you're actually training your kids to use the potty you're doing it indoors, your teaching them to use the potty in your home, but what if your kids were not at home, what if you went out with your kids and there is an urge to pee or poop and since your training them to use the potty you can't wear them diapers, what is going to happen at that moment.

Well the fact is most parents train their kids to use the potty at home and they feel really confident with themselves, but have they ever considered what might happen if they took their kids out? Most parents set aside a full week to train their kids on how to use the potty without going out at all, this sometimes isn't possible because eventually you just have to go out, and even though accidents will happen don't take it as the worst thing that ever happened instead expect the best from it.

In a Car

Potty-training in a car can be quite challenging as the child is away from the familiar environment. Whether you are on a short journey or on a long road trip, it is important to prepare for the inevitable as the child may need to ease themselves at a time you do not expect. Though this situation might be different for you and the child, adaptability is key.

Some parents choose to use diapers when on a road trip. We don't advise you to do this, as it is basically moving back to square one. However, you can use diapers if your child is still very new to potty-training.

There are other ways you can prepare yourself and the child for road trips. First, you should prepare yourself mentally for any possibility. Do not get surprised if the child suddenly says he or she has to pee. Before leaving the house, let the child know you will be going on a ride and encourage them to empty his bowels if he or she needs to do so. Communication is an important aspect of potty-training and it is, therefore, necessary to carry the child along in whatever decision you are about to make.

To continue with the process of potty-training even when in a car, there are some necessary supplies you will need to aid the process if you do not want to use diapers. The first thing you should get is a travel potty, which will be in the car always, along with wipes and disinfectant. You can also use the travel potty in public toilets if you do not want your child to sit on a public toilet. If you have no other choice, get disposable toilet seat covers for extra protection.

Getting disposable bags is also recommended. You can store the child's clothes in them in case of accidents and also use them to dispose of the child's waste. It will also prevent any mess from dropping into the car. Ensure the child is dressed in easily removable clothes in case of an urgent need to go.

Have a clean towel always ready in case of accidents. To reduce the frequency of accidents, make sure you stop at intervals at places such as gas stations or stores to give the child a chance to ease themselves. You can also bring extra clothes, car seat covers, and extra underwear along to be safe.

In a Daycare

Maintaining the potty-training results when a child goes to daycare requires the cooperation of the parent and the daycare provider. The real challenge is the change in environment and bathroom routine.

Most daycares in the past used to offer to help potty train children, but such daycares are hard to find these days, if not non-existent. Most daycares nowadays only accept potty-trained children or prefer to let the child use diapers instead of going commando. You might be tempted as a parent to go back to using diapers, which, however, will be a waste of previous efforts.

You should take a tour of the daycare first to make sure the environment is clean and safe enough for the child. Thoroughly inspect the facilities and ask questions when necessary.

It is important to take time to read the daycare policy and discuss it with the provider before registering your child to prevent issues. After getting a daycare with a suitable potty-training policy, you can now discuss the terms and then sign the agreement.

To make it convenient for both the child and the daycare provider, discuss the potty-training method the child uses at home and the bathroom routine with the provider. You can also discuss the reward system and the usual toilet facilities the child is used to. Also, inform the caregiver that will be in charge of your child about the usual signs that the child is about to go. This is important, as the child may be reluctant to speak to an unfamiliar face.

We advise you to make sure the child is comfortable with the caregiver. Let the child know he can talk to the caregiver if he needs to go.

If your child is only able to use a potty chair at the moment, you can bring the child's potty along if the provider is comfortable with it. Using the same equipment will make it easier for the child to adjust. Bring extra clothes and underwear for the child in case of accidents.

You can request reports and feedback from the provider periodically to know about the child's progress.

Traveling

Sometimes travel cannot be avoided while potty-training, but it is best if you can avoid having to go places while the child is potty-training. If you are to the point where the child is mostly trained, but not completely and it has taken longer to train than you expected, this is where travel tips can help out.

When you leave the house, you want the child to be empty. This is going to limit accidents. Do not provide liquids on the road and go potty before leaving. You want to avoid putting them in training diapers because again, it reinforces the idea that it is ok to have an accident.

Make sure you take the potty chair or adapter seat with you as the child is small and will require lots of stops along the way. Keep an eye out along the way for places to stop so that you are ready if the child has to go to the bathroom.

Have hygiene products ready like tissues and sanitizing gels in case you cannot properly sanitize in a strange bathroom. Keeping toilet paper in the car is not a bad idea either. You do not want to have to get creative with a toddler.

You want to use the stall that is made for handicapped people so you have plenty of room but the seat may be higher than normal so it will require your help. Many places are now incorporating family bathrooms to make room for toddlers and parents so utilize these when you can.

This is a good time to teach more about hygiene. Have the child place toilet paper on the seat of a strange toilet. Safety is important as well so always go with the child to the bathroom. Make sure an adult is around all the time.

Make sure you have some sort of mattress protection with you. This can be a waterproof sheet, plastic tablecloth, plastic bag, or bathroom mat with a rubber back. Just like you don't want the mattress soiled at home, neither does a hotel, friends, or relatives.

It is not uncommon for accidents to occur at this point. If that happens, go back to training pants and enjoy the trip. Start again when you get home. It is too much of an exciting, stressful, fun time to get the child into a routine.

Be aware of the child's diet while traveling. The change in food can create a change in bowel movement frequency and consistency so make sure you are paying attention to that and react accordingly.

In a Public Place

To maintain potty-training results when with your child in a public place, we advise you to create a potty plan before you leave your home. Preparation is key to sustain the progress you've made. You must be mentally prepared as your child may need to use the toilet at any time.

Before leaving the house, let your child ease themselves if he or she needs to. You can try this many times before leaving. If the destination is a familiar place, make a mental note of where the nearest bathroom is or places where you can easily stop along the way, such as gas stations, stores, or restaurants.

When in public, don't get too carried away to pay attention to your child when he needs to use the bathroom. You can develop a safe word or physical signal together with your child which can be used in public to know when the child needs to use the bathroom.

If your child is scared of using public toilets, you can purchase a portable toilet seat cover which you can place on the toilet to make the child feel safe. Toilets with automatic flushing can startle the kid or get the child wet, so use a small piece of tape or any other suitable item to block the motion sensor. There are also other options like the inflatable potty, which is quite affordable and convenient. You should endeavor to have wipes and disinfectant with you whenever you go out with your child. You might need them at any time.

Don't panic if the child shows signs that he or she is about to go or if they say so. Calmly move the child to the nearest bathroom and try to distract them on the way there. Always choose bathrooms that are mostly unoccupied or less noisy.

Keep This in Mind When Handling Potty-Training When Not at Home

Don't Leave the House without Having a Toilet Trip with Your Kids

This might seem kind of obvious but it's important I made mention of it. Ensure your kids visit the potty before leaving the house, even if you're not going very far; ensure they visit the potty every last minute. Turn it into a daily routine, believe me, this will help you and your kids in the future.

Get Your Kids to Use Their Potty in Different Surroundings

If you're planning on going on a trip with your kids or you plan on leaving the house, a day before the outing try making sure your kids make use of the potty in different surroundings or rooms. This actually will help them understand that there's no link between the physical surroundings and their ability to use the potty.

Begin with Short Trips

Alright, so before entering into lots of long ambitious trips, try venturing into short outings with your kids to a more conversant place, it could be a friend's house, your cousins or even a local shop. This is actually going to help your kids develop confidence slowly when out without diapers.

CHAPTER 7:

Urination and Bowel Movements

Urine is one of the principal body-liquids one can excrete like sweat. Girls and boys differ when excreting this waste. To know more about pee here's some basic info.

Parts of the Urinary Tract

When you drink water, the liquid gets to nourish your body. After a few hours, the excess water and waste will leave your body through the urinary tract.

What comprises the urinary tract?

Kidneys

They're two bean-shaped organs located below the ribcage and are responsible for the creation and excretion of urine. They filter blood, remove wastes, and control the fluid balance of the body.

Bladder

It's a sac that collects and holds excess water from the kidney until it's time to release the liquid outside the body. The normal capacity of a bladder is around 400 to 600 ml.

Ureters

These are tubes where the urine passes from the kidney to the bladder. There are two ureters in which the first is located in the abdomen, while the other is in the pelvic region.

Urethra

It's the tube that brings pee from the bladder and out of the male body organ when your child pees. The urethra in men is longer than those of women.

Urination is the process of excreting urine or pee. Excess water and waste are transformed as urine from the kidneys and then stored in the bladders by passing through the ureters. When the body is ready for excretion, the urine will pass the urethra and through the male organ for relief.

What's Pee Made Of?

Pee comprises not just the water your child drinks. It also contains body nutrients and harmful oxidants. But what is it made of? Here are interesting elements of urine:

- Water

- Excess sugar

- Urea

- Urochrome

- Inorganic salts

- Creatinine

- Organic compounds

- Ammonia

- Other metabolites

Urine Color

Pee differs in appearance and color, depending on the person's dehydration level. Healthy urine's color ranges from transparent to pale yellow. But, if it's darker than that, it could hint of underlying illnesses.

- Colorless to pale yellow – healthy and normal

- Yellow to light orange – excess Vitamin B or other medications

- Dark yellow – dehydration

- Pink – excessive consumption of beets

- Red – caused by food tints

- Bloody urine – caused by an underlying disease

There are also green, black, and blue urine caused by disease syndromes or colors of the food one eats. If you're unsure about the health status of your child's urine, you can visit a medical facility and have a urinalysis.

Odor

The odor reflects what your child has consumed. Some odors can be sweet, telltale, or strong. It is often reminiscent of the food one eats.

Healthy Urine in Children

Instilling healthy urination in children will prevent underlying diseases and frequent urination in a child. It involves a couple of safety measures to ensure your toddler is healthy and strong.

If you want to prevent the onset of illnesses, here are the things you need to keep in mind.

- **Maintaining proper hygiene.** If you're potty training your kid, teach him how to wipe properly, especially his genital areas after urinating or having a bowel movement.

- **Avoid soapy water.** Soapy water can cause irritation to the private regions. Avoid buying and using products that have high pH levels too. Bubble baths are also not advisable for younger children.

- **Don't use tight pajamas or underpants.** A loose pajama is a lot better than a tight one because it allows breathability around his genitals. More parents are considering the use of baggy clothes for their children. Some even prefer their child running around naked.

- **Increase water intake.** Water flushes out wastes and bacteria out of your child's body. It boosts energy and relieves fatigue from your child, especially when he's playing or exercising with you. The recommended fluid intake for children ages 1 – 3 years old is 1 liter.

- **Change or remove diapers often.** Now that you're teaching your child how to potty, you'll know why diapers should go "bye-bye." Prolonged use of diapers can cause infection and skin rashes. Toxic chemicals used in the production of diapers can penetrate your child's body system and lower his immunity level.

- **Never hold back pee.** When your child wants to go to the potty, do act immediately. Don't let your child hold back his pee. He must empty his bladder completely to avoid urinary tract infections.

How Your Bowel Works

Poop is something everyone hardly to talk about because it's "Yucky!" However, it's rather important to talk about your bowel movements to ensure living a healthy life. So, how does the bowel process work?

1. It begins when you eat

When you eat, the food comes into contact with your saliva, which breaks down the food chemicals to make it easier to chew and swallow. Your tongue pushes the chewed food toward your throat and through the opening of the esophagus.

2. Down the esophagus

This is the long, muscular tube connecting the throat to the stomach. It's about 10 to 25 centimeters long and runs behind the windpipe and heart organs.

The muscle walls of the esophagus squeeze the food and prod it downwards in a slow manner. About two or three seconds later, the food will reach the stomach to be broken down into a liquid state.

3. Storing in the stomach

After the food travels through the esophagus, it'll reach the bottom of your stomach. The stomach is responsible for storing the food, breaking it into a liquid mixture, and pushing and emptying it into the small intestine.

Meanwhile, the constant churning of the muscle breaks food in a physical matter. The stomach also releases acids responsible for the chemical breakdown of food, while the enzyme pepsin, in the meantime, is in charge of breaking protein particles.

4. Passing through the small intestine

The small intestine is a long tube that further breaks down the food mixture so that the body can absorb the vitamins and nutrients it needed. The small intestine works with the liver, pancreas, and gallbladder to extract these vitamins.

The leftover waste your body does not need will go to the large intestines until it is excreted by the body.

6. Going to the large intestine

After the wastes are separated from the food mixture, it ends up in the large intestines, also known as the colon. Water left in the waste is absorbed until the mixture gets harder and harder. That solid waste is known as stool or poop.

The colon pushes the wastes into the rectum until your body is ready to release them. When you go to the bathroom, the stool goes out of your anus from the rectum.

How to Have a Healthy Bowel Movement

Bowel movement is a significant subject and should not be disregarded as a joke. Any changes in your child's stool can already be a sign of an underlying health issue. Before you begin to worry about your child's regular bowel schedule, know that each kid has his own regular bowel movement.

A child can poop once or twice a day, and it would still be considered normal. Just watch out for constipation and diarrhea in your kid. In order to promote a healthy colon and regular bowel movements, here's what you can do:

Drink More Water

Water can help soften stool and prevent constipation. Also, when you let your child eat fiber-rich foods, it can increase the bulk in the intestines. This leads the colon to contract and push the stool properly. You can let your child drink fruit juice and soup, but water should not be taken out of his diet.

Eat More Fiber

Fiber-rich foods play a vital role in healthy bowel movement. It fills the stomach quickly and speeds up the stool in your digestive system. The best examples of fiber-rich foods are prunes, oatmeal, beans, and spinach.

Avoid Low-Fiber Foods

Limit your child's intake of low-fiber foods like cream, processed snacks, sugary foods, and cheese. These can harden the stool and ultimately lead to constipation.

Don't Tell Your Child to Hold

Never tell your child to resist holding their bowels. It can result in constipation and a much more serious infection due to the bacteria build-up. When your child wants to go and poop, you, as a parent, must address that issue quickly.

Avoid Stress

Stress can cause the colon to spasm, which might result in constipation or diarrhea. Remember, if you're potty training your child, try to take away the strain first. If your kid is still anxious, reassure him about taking potty on his own. Talk to him until it eases his mind.

Don't Use Negative Words to Describe a Bowel Movement

The words, "Yuck," "Stinky," and "Dirty," might have an intense meaning to your child. If you tell him that his stool is yucky and dirty (although slightly true), he can become self-conscious and hesitant to relieve himself. He may think it's bad, and that's why he has to avoid it.

Diarrhea vs. Constipation

These two are the most common problems in bowel movement. They happen when a does not practice healthy bowel missions.

Diarrhea

Diarrhea is when your bowels move too often. They happen to be loose and watery. Diarrhea is caused by the food or medicines your child takes. Too much of it can cause your child to dehydrate.

Diarrhea also starts when a person digests dirty food. That's why food safety procedures during meal times are observed. The food must be thoroughly cooked before serving. Meanwhile, your child should wash his hands before eating to avoid germs that can cause him stomachaches.

When to call a doctor when your child suffers from diarrhea?

If your child has these symptoms, seek professional help straight away:

- When your child is too weak to stand or move

- Suspected dehydration for hours

- Vomits liquids

- Around 10 watery stools within 24 hours

- Bloody stools

- Has fever

Constipation

Constipation is when you're not moving your bowels enough. Your stool happens to be harder and drier than it should be. A regular bowel movement should be soft and quick to pass. If after three to four days, and one still doesn't have any bowel movement, then that's constipation.

How can you tell that your child has constipation?

- The stool is dry and hard

- Your child went by at least three days without pooping

- Difficulty in defecating

- Constrained facial expressions

- Your child is experiencing rectal pain

How to Prevent Constipation

Constipation can be avoided by practicing these tips at home for your child:

- Drink adequate fluids

As parents, make sure that your child is drinking enough fluids. Water intake for children ages 1 to 3 years old should be at least 1 liter. You can also let him drink fruit juices like prune and apple to ease constipation. The added fiber can relieve and soften the stool.

- Gradual switch to breast milk and formula

If you want to shift from breast milk to formula, give your child 1 to 2 fl oz. of water twice a day for two weeks. Follow the suggested measure of feedings while taking extra water in between.

CHAPTER 8:

Errors in Potty Training

Beyond the usual fear of pooping on the toilet, children just don't get used to sitting on the stool, so it may be hard for them to get hanging from it. Help keep your child's body going by giving him plenty of fluids and fruits and vegetables loaded with nutrients. This would make it easier to go to the toilet.

When you note any significant changes in the daily behavior of your child (say he used to poop once a day, and now he isn't pooping), talking about the constipation remedies with your child's doctor. Your doctor may also want to see your child so that there is no other underlying issue. "Often, it just takes a few days to back the training and get your child on track," says Dr. Klemsz. After all, a child can be upset by potty training, which can cause constipation and eventually discomfort as it poops. Take the time, "The framework, potty or toilet, and help must be given, but your child must want to do it," says Dr. Klemsz.

So note, if your child has a lot of stress (such as a recent transfer or a new brother), it will speed up potty training. However, as long as you offer potty training, "for most babies, they'll have a fair shot," says Dr. Klemsz. In the meantime, she gives this sound advice: "Instead of looking at potty training as a challenge, see it as an opportunity for your child to get to know him better—how he learns and how he adapts to stress. You will get a great deal about the character of your child, and the lessons you will learn about your child through potty training will educate her about other challenges.

The Risks of Early Potty Training

There are many reasons why your child should be trained as early as possible. You want to avoid purchasing slides; they're environmentally harmful, costly, and disgusting. You want your child to be in front of the game. There are no-brainer explanations for early potty training. However, in contrast to the size of the reasons you should not, the reasons why you want to train your child early on sound dumb.

According to Dr. Steve Hodges, MD. from the BedwettingAndAccidents.com website, the willingness of children under the age of three to take full responsibility for their toilet activities is irrational.

How Can Early Potty Training Possibly Go Wrong?

Of course, children will undergo potty training well in advance of their age of three, but will they do it properly? (Yes, the right way.) When it comes to using the potty, a mistake can lead to some health issues.

Dr. Hodges states that from the approximately 100 children he sees every week in his clinic, approximately half were potty before the age of three and are so-' dysfunctional voiders,' because of which urinary tract infections, bed weathering and sudden occurrence of accidents (regression) have been caused.

When a child holds poop chronically, a mass forms in the rectum that fills up the space that the bladder uses to retain urine, the nerves may be irritated by the mass and trigger involuntary contractions of the bladder. Unwanted contractions, together with a lack of urinary capacity, frequently cause urination and accidents.

It's getting even stressful. This collection of poo in the rectum includes several bacteria. And those bacteria are very likely to glide over the bladder and trigger bladder infections in children, mainly if they are inclined to pee.

You're not alone if you're cringing about all this pink and poop talk. Some parents think that potty education is healthy and does not bother to mention it to their doctors. Nonetheless, it must be addressed. The prevention of injuries, bed weeding, and bladder infections have been the main focus of recent studies, including this one released by the National Center for Biotechnology Knowledge.

How Are These Problems Related to Early Training?

The reason small children who train potty as early as the age of 2 have more issues than children who wait for at least three years is that they are not mature enough to decide for themselves when they will pee and pee. You do not know yet how necessary it is to remove right when you feel the urge and eliminate it. According to Dr. Hodges, the bladder shrinks every year while retaining urine and is overactive.

What Are You Supposed to Do?

Tell your child every two hours to use the toilet. Don't ask. Don't ask. We are probably too busy to have fun and keep it as long as possible. This is a dangerous habit, which strengthens the bladder to such an extent that the child is desensitized to sensations of fullness, and the bladder empties itself.

Don't bow to the burden of peers. When a school or daycare provider advises you that your child needs potty education before going to school, find another provider.

Remind them to "let it out" before leaving the bathroom. You may be a lucky parent whose child just "gets it" off the fleece. Right, maybe your child is two years old. But remember that you are not alone, with parents still dealing with potty training. Finally, you're in the majority.

You don't trust a baby to brush their teeth every night, and you don't trust a baby to know how to extract them every time you use your shower. Recall early potty training can extend your duty to track your bathroom habits closely.

Additional potty training resources: risks of early potty training interaction of the toilet age and incomplete voiding.

Potty training should be a tried-and-tested experience for both the child and the parents. Progress typically does not occur without accidents—and potentially tears or other setbacks—on the road. Understanding how to use the toilet does not suit any effort in one size. Whatever your potty training experience, it is essential to ensure that your child feels comfortable and that you express a positive attitude when learning this new skill.

While positivity is the answer, you need to know those "don't"—and avoid falling into them. Below are some of the most common well-meaning yet ultimately ineffective pitfalls for clearing your child while training potty.

Do not push the issue. Make sure that your child can use the pot before training begins. A child who can express his needs demonstrates interest in bathroom independence and is capable of meeting physical needs such as shoes, knowing when "they need to go," and following a series of necessary steps is common signs of preparation.

If your child refuses to leave, it may create a negative atmosphere to force them to go and sit on the pot and eventually lead to more resistance. This can create detrimental associations with using the bathroom that can be difficult to eliminate and create your child to refrain from urination, which can be harmful.

Often seek to provide support and encouragement. If the process becomes a fight, even if your child seems "ready," otherwise, you could consider braking. If you are both excited about this "big baby" move, you will get the best results (with potty training and relationship).

Try to treat this phase of learning just as you do with other milestones such as sit, walk, and speak. Honor, though almost all children arrive there, others need a little more time and maturity to master these skills.

You should not start training during a time of stress. Even good stress is weak stress when it comes to potty training. Marriages, new children, vacations, guests, and vacations will trouble your child–including the difficulties of coping with divorce, death, or moving to a new home.

If something new and significant is on the horizon of your life, rethink potty training right now. Wait before life settles, and the healthy activity flow begins again. It gives your child protection and allows them to position toilets alongside other regular routines quickly. Moreover, you will receive more focus and positive energy to help your child recover from the pains.

Don't set deadlines. Young children sometimes aren't working well within periods and don't have the same time definition as adults. Keep the potty training goals practical. Or, better yet, drive them out the window. Know that potty children train at different levels and ages. Some children learn before eighteen months but may take another year to a few years before they are ready. Just before kindergarten, some don't master the skill. While some kids train the toilet quickly, it's a much longer process for others.

Programs that pledge that in three days, a day, or even 100 days, your child will receive potty training; do not take into consideration your child's individuality. And the child has its unique personality and development goals and brings various skills to the table, and there is no clear one-size-fit solution.

Programs operating on schedule frequently recommend corrective interventions, or are inflexible or train parents, instead of the kid. This sets the deadline for a feeling of disappointment and lots of unhealthy tension for a lot of parents and children.

However, the many diverse social households, including working parents, households with loads of children, children with special needs, multiples, and parents with custody, cannot be taken into account. Make sure that every approach you use is versatile and meets everyone's needs. Particularly, choose a potty training strategy that will encourage your child to feel comfortable, no matter whether it takes a few days or several months.

Don't view accidents as a big deal. One of the cornerstones of useful and productive potty training models is to remember: "It's a regular part of life." Make your child more confident: going to a bathroom—and the sometimes occurring accident—is inevitable and nothing to feel terrible about. Accidents happen, and as part of the planned process, we learn from them.

In reality, overemphasis on accidents can exacerbate misfortunes or feelings of shame, which lead to more accidents. If they arise, keep the tone calm and slow, or even arrogant. Recruit your child in the clean-up and proceed to the next opportunity to use the potty.

Don't wear clothing that is hard to deal with an instructor who is in charge of a group of potty trainees who can tell you how difficult buttons (snaps, zips, socks, overalls, several layers and several other unmanageable clothes) can be controlled for little arms and hands.

Make it as convenient for your child as possible. Use the child's motor skills as a guide when choosing potty clothing. Simple pants, shorts, or skirts in the elastic waist are ideal for most people.

CHAPTER 9:

Learn How to Talk Potty language

When it comes to potty training, parents tend to wonder what terms they need to use with their children. Is it appropriate to use terms like urine or bowel movement, or should you use more casual words like pee and poop?

To Use Correct or Cute Language

Whether you use the clinically correct word for a body part and waste is pretty much up to you and typically involves your family history. Parents who had parents that used poop and pee will likely use the same terms with their children. There isn't anything wrong with either. You aren't going to be hurting your child if you use childish words to describe these things. They are a child, and unless you are planning are keeping them hidden away, they are going to eventually learn the right terms and also some slang that is probably going to cause you to cringe. Calling his penis, a "wee wee" now isn't going to affect that.

Likewise, there is plenty of room to use the proper terms now if you would like to. By providing them with both of the words, you may believe that you are going to confuse them, but the opposite is true. You're providing them with different ways to express themselves and lots of vocabulary to do so when they need to. Mom and Dad can use separate potty language if they want.

If your child is in daycare, you can ask their teacher what type of potty language they use and stick to that if you want. That can help to get rid of any confusion between the adults, but, again, you don't have to be rigid about picking the "right" words.

Potty Language Shouldn't Be a Source of Shame

Confusion will happen if you choose to discourage or eliminate certain words or give words a negative emotion. If you are uncomfortable with a word that your spouse may use, you may want to take a moment to figure out why. Do you think the word is embarrassing or feel shame about words even though they aren't cursed words and most people would find them appropriate for public use? You can easily convey this attitude to your child, especially if you tend to argue with your spouse about it or correct them around your child.

You need to make sure that your child feels comfortable talking about every aspect of using the bathroom around you, and they will likely find it easier and more comfortable to say, "poo-poo, it hurts," instead of "I'm having difficulty with my bowel movement." This is especially true when their language skills aren't strong yet.

Potty Language Should Be G Rated

If the words that you or your spouse uses are inappropriate, and you wouldn't use them around your peers, such as other moms with toddlers, then you should probably find more appropriate words. There isn't anything cute or developmentally appropriate about teaching your child a swear word. And it is also very hard to teach your toddler that it is okay to say one word at home, but they can't use it in public.

If your child has already started to use words that would garner an R-rating, put a stop to it as soon as you can and do your best to ignore this action in your child. It can be very tempting to make a huge deal out of banning a word or giving it a scary label, but this will typically make the problem worse and makes it more alluring to your toddler to use it. Forbidden fruit tastes the sweetest.

What Goes into the Toilet?

Urine is the fluid that is created by the kidneys after they have cleaned your blood. This liquid waste travels from the kidneys and into the bladder and leaves the body through the urethra. Most adults don't use the word urethra. For boys, the urethra is the tube that passes through the penis. In girls, it empties out in the space in front of the vagina, so it can't be easily seen. There are, in fact, a lot of adult women who don't even know exactly where their pee comes out. The act of emptying the bladder is known as urination.

The term excrement or feces refers to the solid waste that travels through the intestinal tract and out the rectum. This is what is left over once the body has removed everything it needs from food. Defecation is the act of emptying the bowels.

There are a lot of other proper and slang words that can be used to describe what gets put into the toilet. Your family probably already has its own favorites. You may also find that once you start talking about the potty with your child, they will have this constant stream of "potty talk" that you will have to deal with. We'll talk about that in a minute.

To help you figure out what word to use, here are some proper and slang words for urination and defecation:

- Pee or pee-pee

- Tinkle

- Wee or wee-wee

- Number one

- BM

- Number two

- Poop

- Doo-doo

There are just as many words that can be used to describe the room where the toilet is. You may be using a potty for your child that you keep in a different space during their training, but they should know what they need to call the room when they are somewhere else. Some words are: Washroom, Toilet, Little girls' or little boys' room, Restroom, Bathroom

You are also going to need to come up with potty words when talking about body parts. A boy will be able to see pee coming out of his penis. You can call it a penis, or you can call it a pee-pee, or a completely different word. However, you should probably use the right word from the start, and not refer to it using a word that you would not want your child to say. They are going to hear slang at some point, but you shouldn't teach it to them now.

The important thing is to make sure you keep your potty words simples. Avoid using words that you don't want them to use. And you should make sure that everybody involved in the potty training knows what to use.

Conclusion

You are now armed with information related to potty training. I hope it has been interesting and helpful, and that you feel confident and prepared to begin your own early potty learning journey.

I warmly encourage you to share your newfound knowledge with other interested parents and spread the word about the many merits of this approach.

Let's hope it was informative and able to provide you with all of the tools you need to achieve your goals whatever they may be. With your investment of time and a little preparation, you will be ready to start off on the potty-training journey with your little one. I wish you much success in your efforts.

Don't forget to use all the tools at your disposal. Be silly, have fun, read books, sing songs – all of these things are part of your child's normal daily routine; they instill a sense of enjoyment in learning new things and help to make it easier to master a skill or take on a new challenge. If it becomes a chore, it will quickly be ignored, and you will find more accidents occurring in favor of extra playtime or just plain old defiance. Keeping things lighthearted also helps tremendously if, and when, an accident does come along. Be a consistent cheerleader for your little one, and you will see success follows quickly.

It is especially important to include yourself in the journey. Don't be caught up in stigmas. It is OK to talk about pooping, peeing, and farting. It really isn't a big deal to discuss bathroom habits. And don't be too shy to be your child's mentor. Children learn by seeing and repeating. This type of mimicking actually helps them to understand what is expected of them, not only when it comes to using the potty but also good manners, proper table etiquette, and so much more. You are one of the most important keys to your child's success in life and especially in potty training.

The next step depends on you. If you are just starting off or in the early stages of preparation, take your time, and be sure that your child is really ready. Set your own pace and don't let it get you down if you come across a setback or regression. Children are resilient, and you need to be too. Even when your child is "fully" trained, accidents can happen.

I wish you the best of luck for an exciting and enjoyable period of potty training. You will also want to keep in mind that your ultimate goal for your child is about more than just potty training. It is about helping your child learn, grow, and adapt to the world we live in. Potty training is just one more milestone, one more task to master, and your child will be so proud to say "I go potty."

www.ingramcontent.com/pod-product-compliance
Lightning Source LLC
Chambersburg PA
CBHW061001050726
47592CB00003B/1297